# PUDDINGS

# PUDDINGS

## Sweet & Savory Puddings, Custards, Flans & Mousses

### Marie Simmons

Photography by David Lazarus
Calligraphy by Richard High

HOUGHTON MIFFLIN COMPANY
BOSTON    NEW YORK
1999

For information about permission to reproduce selections from this book,
write to Permissions, Houghton Mifflin Company, 215 Park Avenue South,
New York, New York 10003.

Library of Congress Cataloging-in-Publication Data
Simmons, Marie.
Puddings A to Z : sweet and savory puddings, custards, flans & mousses / Marie Simmons ;
photography by David Lazarus ; calligraphy by Richard High.
p.  cm.
ISBN 0-395-90990-2
1. Puddings. I. Title.
TX773.S522  1999                                                          99-32150
                                                                                              CIP

Printed and bound in Italy

Designed by Susan McClellan

Front cover: Crème Caramel with Orange Zest & Spices (page 26) by David Lazarus
Food stylist: Susan Ehlich
Prop stylist: Francine Matalon-Degni

SFE 10 9 8 7 6 5 4 3 2 1

**For Mom and Aunt Tess**

# Acknowledgments

ABOUT THE SAME TIME that I began work on this book, my husband was offered a job in San Francisco. Soon I found myself reluctantly transporting my kitchen from the East Coast to the West. Once I had unpacked my cooking gear and filled the house with the aroma of bread pudding, my resistance to the move began to subside.

I would like to thank my new neighbors on Montell Street in Oakland, California, for their enthusiastic acceptance of the lady with the puddings. I wish to thank as well many other new California friends: Jane Ellison; Caryle Levine and Ken Lee; Paula, Edward, Jeffrey and Julia Hamilton; Linda Carucci and Al Rehmke; Weezie and Howard Mott; Debbie and Peter Rugh; Kasma Loha-unchit and Michael Babcock; Craig de Fonzo and Emily Brown de Fonzo; Louise Walker; Sharna Hoffman; Jim Mellgren and Sydney Turnshek; Ann Segerstrom; Gary Danko; Joanne Weir; Hilary Chalmers; Nancy Kux and so many others for their warm welcomes. A great big thank-you to Sudie Coleman, who carefully retested all the recipes, offering invaluable culinary suggestions and lots of moral support, to Ellye Bloom, Dana Jacobi and Shirley King for pudding research, to David Lazarus and Susan Ehlich for the beautiful photographs, to my agent Judith Weber, to my editor Rux Martin and my publisher Barry Estabrook at Houghton Mifflin, to Susan McClellan for her design, to Lori Galvin-Frost and Wendy Ruopp for editing assistance, to John, my husband, who is the star among pudding tasters as far as I am concerned, and to Mom and Aunt Tess for their inspiration.

## M *is for*

Mango Pudding with Blueberries   55

Malted-Milk Chocolate Pudding   58

## N *is for*

Nadia's Russian Cream Dessert with Red Plum Sauce   59

## O *is for*

Onion Custards   61

## P *is for*

Pistachio Pots de Crème   63

Polenta Pudding with Creamy Fig Sauce   65

## Q *is for*

Queen of Puddings   67

## R *is for*

Ricotta Pudding with Strawberry Sauce   69

## S *is for*

Savory Corn Pudding   71

Steamed Ginger & Cranberry Pudding   74

# Introduction

*Blessed be he that invented pudding, for it is a Manna*
*that hits the Palates of all Sorts of People . . .*
—Henri deValbourg (1698)

IF I HAD COME UPON THE OBSERVATION of the appreciative Frenchman when I was a child, I might have committed it to memory on the spot and recited it at bedtime right after my prayers, for pudding was my favorite food. It still is.

It was also one of the first foods I remember "helping" my mother make. I stood on a chair so I could see into the pot, while Mom stirred together the milk and the gray-brown mix from the My T Fine box. As we took turns with the wooden spoon, the thin, drab liquid soon began to turn into thick, dark, sumptuously creamy chocolate pudding. I watched in anticipation as Mom poured it into small dishes. "But I can't wait," I would whine, when she warned it would burn my mouth. Knowing that words alone wouldn't placate me, she handed me the stirring spoon. Slowly, carefully, I licked it systematically, making roads in the glossy coating, until the spoon was sparkling clean.

Today, I make chocolate pudding from scratch, not from a boxed mix, but I still lick the spoon. Choosing real ingredients is more than grown-up snobbery, it's a matter of taste. As I stir chocolate, sugar, cornstarch and milk together and remove the pan from the heat moments later, the quivery chocolate taking shape is proof that homemade pudding is just as easy and fast as the packaged kind—and much more delicious. Pudding is "manna" all right, but a big part of its lasting appeal comes from the fact that it's manna from the basics: eggs, sugar, milk—and sometimes bread, rice, noodles, tapioca, cornmeal or even Grape-Nuts.

The family of puddings is more various than these simple ingredients would seem to dictate. Eggs, sugar and milk cooked on top of the stove or baked in the oven turn into custard. Baked and covered with a sauce of caramelized sugar, the same ingredients make flan. With whipped cream folded in, custard becomes mousse. Mousse made with gelatin is known as Bavarian cream. When heavy cream and more egg yolks are added, custard is transformed into pot de crème. Dressed up with a thin layer of brown sugar broiled into a crackling coating, pot de crème is transformed into crème brûlée, the most popular restaurant dessert of all.

Bread soaked in the custard and baked becomes bread pudding. Take the bread, layer it with fresh berries in a bowl, soak it with the sweetened berry juices and pile on whipped cream, and the whole swells into summer pudding. And when ladyfingers or sponge cake replace the bread and are sprinkled with liqueur and covered with custard, bread pudding is elevated into diplomat pudding, a stunning dessert for holiday entertaining even if you don't have any diplomats on your guest list.

Then there are the desserts that are part cake, part pudding, like clafouti and sticky toffee pudding, which are more cakey, and sponge pudding, which separates miraculously into a top layer of cake and a bottom layer of dreamy sauce that can be scooped out with every serving. All these permutations may account for the confusing British tendency to call all dessert "pudding"—with so many variations, who can blame them!

THE EARLIEST PUDDINGS, however, were not sweet but savory. The word itself derives from the French *boudin,* or sausage. These dishes were made from animal blood, mixed with bread crumbs, oatmeal or other fillers, suet and lots of spices, or from animal organs, well seasoned and stuffed into containers or casings. Sometimes the mixtures were wrapped in a cloth and steamed over a simmering pot of stew. From these humble origins sprang the great British tradition of the steamed pudding, like the flaming pudding in Charles Dickens' *A Christmas Carol.* The most famous descendant of the savory pudding is the Scottish national dish, haggis, which consists of parts of a sheep ground with spices and grain, stuffed into the animal's stomach and boiled.

History aside, you will find no stuffed stomachs (except perhaps your own) in this little book. But there are other puddings of a savory persuasion, including an airy soufflélike corn pudding and a delicate zucchini and Parmesan custard.

As for sweet puddings, my alphabetic interpretations should "hit the palates" of old and young alike, from the stay-at-home cook to the restaurant-going sophisticate.

## Pudding Wisdom

These simple techniques will make all your puddings go smoothly.

**Tempering:** Never add egg yolks directly to a hot mixture or they may curdle and overcook. Instead, first stir a small amount of hot liquid into the yolks to temper them. The warmed yolks can then be added to the hot liquid.

**Straining:** All puddings made with an egg or gelatin base should be strained. Eggs contain a cord that attaches the yolk to the white, which can make a custard or sauce lumpy. Similarly, straining ensures that you won't find lumpy granules of undissolved gelatin in the finished pudding.

**Baking in a water bath:** Setting the custard cup, soufflé dish or pudding dish in a shallow pan half filled with hot water before baking insulates the delicate egg-thickened mixture against the heat, preventing curdling, weeping, cracked top or other signs of overcooking.

**Low-temperature cooking:** Puddings should always be cooked over low heat and stirred gently to prevent scorching. For stovetop puddings, use a heavy pot with a thick, well-insulated bottom. A flame-tamer is also helpful to make the heat less intense. Egg-based pudding should be cooked until an instant-read thermometer registers 165° to 170°F.

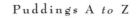

# Apple Butter Bread Pudding with Spiced Apple Cider Sauce

I LOVE THE IDEA OF APPLE BUTTER, but I tire of it as a spread for my morning toast long before the jar is empty. Bread pudding gives apple butter a new lease on life. Spread it lavishly on the bread and make "sandwiches" with it before soaking the bread in the custard. The intense flavor of the cider sauce brings out the mellow taste of the apple butter.

6   slices thin-sliced firm bread,
    crusts trimmed
    About ¾ cup apple butter
2   tablespoons unsalted butter, melted
2   cups milk
4   large eggs
⅓   cup sugar

2   teaspoons vanilla extract
½   teaspoon ground cinnamon

    Cinnamon Sugar (page 16)
    Spiced Apple Cider Sauce (page 16),
        Cinnamon Custard Sauce (page 17)
    or heavy cream

1. Spread 3 slices of the bread with the apple butter, distributing evenly. Top with the remaining 3 slices of bread. Lightly brush a 1½-quart soufflé dish or other round deep casserole dish with some of the melted butter. Brush the top layer of bread with the remaining butter.

2. Cut each apple butter sandwich into nine (3 across and 3 down) 1-inch squares. Place all the bread in the soufflé dish.

3. In a large bowl, whisk together the milk, eggs, sugar, vanilla and cinnamon until thoroughly blended. Pour over the bread and press down lightly with the back of a spoon or spatula. Let stand for 1 hour, pressing down often so the bread absorbs the custard evenly and doesn't float to the top.

4. Preheat the oven to 350°F, with a rack in the center. Heat a kettle of water to boiling. Set the soufflé dish in a larger baking pan. Place the baking pan in the oven and add enough boiling water to come halfway up the sides of the soufflé dish.

5. Bake until the pudding is puffed and browned and a skewer inserted in the center comes out clean, about 45 minutes. Remove from the oven and let cool in the water bath. Sprinkle the top generously with the cinnamon sugar. Serve warm or at room temperature, with the cider sauce or one of the other suggested toppings.

MAKES 6 SERVINGS

# Cinnamon Sugar

½  cup sugar                    1  teaspoon ground cinnamon

Combine the sugar and cinnamon and stir to blend. Store in a sugar shaker, plastic container or jar, and keep on hand for toast, breakfast cereal or pudding recipes.

# Spiced Apple Cider Sauce

5  cups apple cider                6  whole cloves
1  cup sugar                       1  cinnamon stick (3 inches)
1  strip (2 x ½ inch) orange zest  1  inch vanilla bean or 1 teaspoon
1  strip (2 x ½ inch) lemon zest      vanilla extract

In a medium saucepan, combine the cider, sugar, zests, cloves, cinnamon stick and vanilla bean, if using. (Do not add the vanilla extract now.) Heat to boiling and boil over medium to medium-high heat until the cider is reduced by half, about 25 minutes. Set a sieve over a small bowl and strain out and discard the solids. Add the vanilla extract, if using. Serve warm or cold as a sauce for the pudding.

MAKES ABOUT 2 CUPS

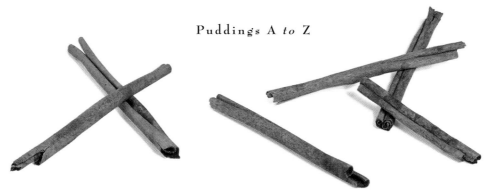

# Cinnamon Custard Sauce

1½ **cups milk**
1 **cinnamon stick (3 inches)**
3 **large egg yolks**

¼ **cup sugar**
½ **teaspoon vanilla extract**

1. Combine the milk and cinnamon stick in a small saucepan and heat until small bubbles appear around the edges. Remove from the heat. Let stand, covered, for 1 hour.

2. Whisk the egg yolks and sugar in a medium bowl until well blended. Remove the cinnamon stick from the milk and gradually stir the milk into the egg mixture. Return to the saucepan and cook over medium-low heat, stirring gently, until the mixture coats the back of a spoon and reaches 165° to 170°F; do not boil. Set a sieve over a small bowl and strain the custard. Stir in the vanilla. Refrigerate until ready to serve. Serve warm. (Reheat in a small, heavy saucepan over low heat, stirring constantly, until warmed.)

MAKES ABOUT 2 CUPS

**Vanilla Custard Sauce:** Omit the cinnamon stick and substitute 1 vanilla bean, split, in step 1. Remove the vanilla bean and scrape the seeds into the sauce mixture with the tip of a sharp knife. Discard the pod. Continue as directed.

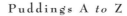

# Basmati Rice Pudding with Coconut Milk

REMINISCENT OF EVERYTHING that is exotic and seductive about India, this pudding has enticing flavors and aromas. As it simmers with the spices, the basmati rice fills the house with its nutty fragrance. The pudding is rich with coconut milk and a drizzle of delicate saffron cream and is garnished with chopped pistachios. If possible, use imported basmati rice or look for something called *kalijira* (sometimes called *gobindovog*), a baby basmati imported from India. It's available from Gold Mine Natural Foods in San Diego (800-475-3663).

| | |
|---|---|
| 3 | whole cardamom pods |
| 1 | whole cinnamon stick (3 inches) |
| 1 | whole clove |
| ½ | teaspoon salt |
| ⅔ | cup imported basmati, kalijira, texmati or kasmati rice |
| ¼ | cup raisins (dark or golden) |

| | |
|---|---|
| 1 | cup canned unsweetened coconut milk, stirred until smooth |
| 1 | cup whole milk |
| 2 | tablespoons packed light brown sugar |
| ½ | cup sweetened flaked coconut |
| ¼-½ | cup heavy cream |
| | Saffron Cream (page 20) |
| 3 | tablespoons chopped pistachios |

1. Combine 1½ cups water, the cardamom, cinnamon stick, clove and salt in a medium saucepan. Heat to boiling. Stir in the rice, reduce the heat to low, cover and cook until tender, about 15 minutes. Drain any excess liquid.

2. Meanwhile, place the raisins in a small bowl and pour ½ cup boiling water over them. Let stand for 15 minutes. When the rice is cooked, add the coconut milk, milk and brown sugar to the rice; stir to blend. Drain the raisins and add them to the rice; heat to boiling. Cover and cook over low heat, stirring occasionally, until the pudding is very thick, about 20 minutes.

3. Stir in the coconut. Add enough heavy cream to thin the pudding, stirring gently. Serve warm or at room temperature. (The pudding will stiffen as it cools; add more heavy cream or milk, 1 tablespoon at a time, to thin the pudding to the desired consistency.) Serve the pudding Indian-style with the whole spices still in it. Spoon into dessert dishes and drizzle with saffron cream. Sprinkle with the chopped pistachios.

**MAKES 6 SERVINGS**

# Saffron Cream

¼ **teaspoon saffron threads**
1 **cup heavy cream**

1 **tablespoon sugar**

Heat the saffron in a small, heavy saucepan just until it takes on a slightly darker color, about 10 seconds. Add the cream and sugar and heat until the cream boils; immediately remove from the heat. Cover and steep for 15 minutes. Place a sieve over a small bowl and strain out the saffron and discard. Refrigerate the cream until chilled. Serve over the pudding.

# Breakfast Pudding

U NLIKELY THOUGH IT MAY SOUND to the uninitiated, this pudding is nourishing, filling and the perfect comfort food. Because it improves upon standing, it is best served the day after it is made. In fact, it is a great dish to make ahead and then eat all week (or all weekend) for breakfast instead of plain cereal. This recipe is from my friend, the late cookbook author Richard Sax. Serve plain or with sliced bananas or other fresh fruit and a drizzle of milk or cream.

| | |
|---|---|
| 1    quart milk, warmed | ½    teaspoon ground cinnamon |
| 1    cup Grape-Nuts |      Pinch of salt |
| 4    large eggs | 1    teaspoon vanilla extract |
| ¾    cup sugar | ⅓    cup raisins |

1. Preheat the oven to 325°F, with a rack in the center. Heat a kettle of water to boiling. Lightly butter a 2-quart casserole or soufflé dish. Set in a larger baking pan.

2. Heat the milk in a large saucepan until small bubbles appear around the edges. Stir in the Grape-Nuts. Remove from the heat and let stand for 15 minutes.

3. Combine the eggs, sugar, cinnamon, salt and vanilla in a large bowl; whisk until blended. Stir in the Grape-Nuts mixture and add the raisins. Pour into the baking dish. Place the baking pan in the oven and carefully add enough boiling water to come halfway up the sides of the casserole or soufflé dish.

4. Bake until the pudding is set, about 1 hour, stirring after 20 minutes and then 20 minutes after that to redistribute the raisins and Grape-Nuts. Remove from the oven and let cool in the water bath. Serve cold, at room temperature or reheated in the microwave.

MAKES **8** TO **10** SERVINGS

# Butterscotch Pudding

H EAVEN IN A CUSTARD CUP is the way I feel about butterscotch. This recipe has just the right amount of butter taste, without being too thick on the lips. Once you have tasted the simple magic of real butterscotch, you'll never go back to the packaged variety.

| | |
|---|---|
| 6 large egg yolks | ¾ cup milk |
| 1 cup heavy cream | 1 teaspoon vanilla extract |
| ⅓ cup packed dark brown sugar | |
| 4 tablespoons unsalted butter, cut into pieces | ½ cup heavy cream, chilled |

1. In the top of a double boiler, whisk the egg yolks until blended; set aside. Heat the cream in a small saucepan until hot; do not boil. Keep warm.

2. Place the brown sugar and butter in a large, heavy skillet. Heat, stirring, until the butter melts and the mixture bubbles. Cook, stirring, over medium-low heat for 2 minutes. Add the warm cream all at once. (It will bubble up a bit.) Remove the skillet from the heat and stir the mixture with a heatproof rubber spatula, scraping the bottom of the skillet and stirring until the mixture stops bubbling. Add the milk.

3. Whisk the butterscotch mixture into the egg yolks until blended. Cook over gently simmering water, stirring gently but constantly, until the pudding thickens enough to coat the back of a spoon and reaches 165° to 170°F, about 15 minutes; do not boil. Remove from the heat.

4. Place a sieve over a large heat-resistant bowl and strain the pudding into the bowl. Add the vanilla and stir to blend. Pour the pudding into four 5-ounce custard cups, distributing evenly. Cool to room temperature. Cover and refrigerate until chilled and set, about 4 hours or overnight.

5. Beat the chilled cream with an electric mixer until it forms soft peaks. Serve the pudding with a dollop of whipped cream.

MAKES 4 SERVINGS

# Berry Fool

FRUIT FOOLS are among the simplest of puddings, with a long history that goes as far back as perhaps the sixteenth century. As we know it today, a fool is a lightly blended mixture of pureed or mashed cooked fruit folded into whipped cream so that the fruit streaks the cream. Adding crème fraîche (a matured thickened cream with a tangy, slightly nutty taste, available at some specialty grocers), sour cream or yogurt gives the cream a nice tart edge, which balances the sweetness of the fruit and the heavy cream. Plan ahead when making this pudding, since the fruit mixture needs to cool before it is folded into the cream.

1   pint strawberries, rinsed and hulled
½   pint blackberries, rinsed and drained
½   pint raspberries, rinsed and drained
⅔   cup sugar
1   tablespoon fresh lime or lemon juice,
     or to taste

1   cup heavy cream, well chilled
⅔   cup crème fraîche, sour cream or
     plain whole-milk yogurt

1. Slice 1 or 2 strawberries and place in a small bowl along with 4 blackberries and 4 raspberries. Set aside, covered and refrigerated, as a garnish.

2. Quarter the remaining strawberries and puree in a food processor. Transfer to a medium saucepan. Add the remaining blackberries and raspberries to the food processor and puree. Press through a sieve to remove the seeds. Add the sieved berries to the saucepan. Stir in the sugar. Cook, stirring, over medium-low heat, until the mixture boils. Boil gently over low heat, stirring often, until the mixture is thickened and mounds slightly on a spoon, about 15 minutes. Remove from the heat and transfer to a heatproof bowl. Stir in the lime or lemon juice. Refrigerate until well chilled, about 3 hours or overnight.

3. Just before serving, whip the heavy cream until soft peaks form. In a small bowl, stir the crème fraîche, sour cream or yogurt until smooth. Add to the whipped cream and gently fold to combine. Add the cream mixture to the chilled berry puree. Gently fold, not thoroughly incorporating, until cream is marbled with the fruit puree. Spoon into individual dessert glasses or a serving bowl, preferably glass. Refrigerate until well chilled, at least 2 hours. The fool is best served the same day. Before serving, garnish with the reserved berries.

**Makes 6 servings**

# Crème Caramel
# with Orange Zest & Spices

W HEN THESE DELICATELY SPICED glossy custards are turned out, the caramelized sugar on the bottom will have melted into a lovely orange-and-caramel-flavored syrup. Make them at least one day before serving so they are thoroughly chilled. For a less rich custard, omit the two egg yolks and use low-fat milk.

| | | | |
|---|---|---|---|
| 2 | cups milk | ¾ | cup sugar |
| 3 | strips (2 x ½ inch) orange zest | 2 | large eggs |
| 2 | whole cloves | 2 | large egg yolks |
| 1 | cinnamon stick (3 inches) | 1 | teaspoon vanilla extract |

1. Combine the milk, 1 of the orange strips, the cloves and the cinnamon stick in a small saucepan. Heat until small bubbles appear around the edges. Remove from the heat, cover and let stand for 20 minutes.

2. Meanwhile, cut the remaining 2 orange strips into long slivers and distribute among six 5-ounce custard cups. Combine ½ cup of the sugar and 2 tablespoons water in a small, heavy skillet. Stir over low heat until the sugar dissolves. Boil, without stirring, until the sugar

turns golden, swirling the pan gently instead of stirring, for about 7 minutes. Pour the caramel into the custard cups over the orange peel, dividing evenly.

3. Preheat the oven to 350°F, with a rack in the center. Heat a kettle of water to boiling. Arrange the custard cups in a 13-x-9-inch baking pan.

4. Place a sieve over a small bowl, strain the milk and discard the solids. In a medium bowl, whisk the eggs, yolks, the remaining ¼ cup sugar and vanilla until thoroughly blended. Gradually stir in the warm milk. Strain the mixture and let stand until the bubbles on top subside. Pour the custard over the caramel in the cups, distributing evenly.

5. Place the baking pan in the oven. Add enough boiling water to come halfway up the sides of the cups. Bake until the custards are set on the edges and still a little shaky in the center, about 30 minutes. Remove from the oven and let cool in the water bath. When the custards are cooled, cover each with plastic wrap and refrigerate until chilled, 8 hours or overnight.

6. Loosen the edges of the custards, using the tip of a knife. Place a serving plate over each cup and invert, shaking the crème caramel loose and letting caramel drip over the custard.

**MAKES 6 SERVINGS**

# Cappuccino Bavarian Cream

B AVARIAN CREAM is similar to mousse, except that it is usually thickened with gelatin and unmolded when set. The deep taste of espresso makes this version a very grown-up dessert. Make it early in the day before serving or, better yet, make it a day ahead.

| | | | |
|---|---|---|---|
| 1 | envelope plus 1 teaspoon unflavored gelatin | ½ | cup sugar |
| 2 | cups half-and-half | 1 | teaspoon vanilla extract |
| 2 | tablespoons instant espresso powder | 1 | cup heavy cream, chilled |
| 4 | egg yolks | 1 | milk chocolate bar, for chocolate curls |

1. Place 3 tablespoons cold water in a small bowl. Sprinkle with the gelatin and set aside to soften.

2. Heat the half-and-half in a medium saucepan until small bubbles appear around the edges. Stir in the espresso powder until dissolved. Meanwhile, whisk the egg yolks and sugar in a medium bowl until blended. Gradually whisk in some of the hot half-and-half, stirring to dissolve the sugar. Stir the mixture back into the hot half-and-half. Cook over low heat, stirring constantly, until the mixture thickens slightly, lightly coats the back of a spoon and reaches 165° to 170°F; do not boil. Remove from the heat. Add the softened gelatin and stir to dissolve.

3. Set a sieve over a medium bowl and strain the custard mixture; add the vanilla. Set the bowl in a larger bowl and surround with ice cubes. Chill the custard, stirring often, until it begins to thicken and mounds slightly, about 15 minutes. Replenish the ice as it melts.

4. Beat the cream in a clean bowl with an electric mixer until soft peaks form. Add to the chilled custard and gently fold together until thoroughly blended. Pour into a 3-to-4-cup mold or a small, deep bowl. Cover and refrigerate for at least 4 hours or overnight.

5. To serve, quickly dip the mold or bowl in hot water. Loosen the edges of the custard, using the tip of a knife. Place a serving plate on top and invert, shaking the Bavarian cream loose.

6. To make the chocolate curls, make sure the chocolate bar is at room temperature or warm it up by holding it, still wrapped, in your hand. Pressing down hard with a vegetable peeler, pare curls of chocolate from the bar and let them fall over the surface of the Bavarian cream.

MAKES 6 TO 8 SERVINGS

# Classic Cherry Clafouti

CLAFOUTI (pronounced kla-foo-TEE) is a popular French dessert that is part pudding and part pancake. Typically it is made with unpitted cherries, but I much prefer to pit the cherries using my handy cherry pitter. The batter is very easy to put together. Like a crepe or pancake batter, it is mostly eggs and milk with just a little flour and sugar. Once you've tried clafouti, you are likely to make it all summer long, as it adapts easily to most summer fruits, including sliced peaches or nectarines, halved figs or apricots, blueberries, raspberries and strawberries. It can even be prepared with seedless grapes, sliced apples or pears. It's best served warm.

¼ cup plus 2 tablespoons sugar

12 ounces dark sweet cherries, rinsed and pitted (about 2 cups)

1½ cups milk

1 cup heavy cream

4 large eggs

1 teaspoon vanilla extract

1 cup all-purpose flour

¼ teaspoon salt

1 tablespoon unsalted butter, cut into small pieces

Superfine or regular sugar for topping

Whipped cream for topping (optional)

1. Preheat the oven to 350°F, with a rack in the center. Generously butter a 10-inch pie plate or other shallow baking dish. Sprinkle evenly with 1 tablespoon of the sugar.

2. Spread the cherries in the pie plate, and sprinkle with 1 tablespoon of the sugar; set aside. Whisk the milk, cream, eggs and vanilla in a medium bowl until blended. Sift the flour, the remaining ¼ cup sugar and the salt into a separate medium bowl.

3. Gradually whisk the milk mixture into the flour mixture until blended. Place a sieve over the empty bowl and strain the batter, pressing on any lumps of flour to dissolve. Pour the batter over the cherries. Dot the top with the small pieces of butter.

4. Bake until the edges are puffed and golden brown and the clafouti is cooked in the center, 45 to 55 minutes. Transfer to a wire rack and sprinkle the top generously with sugar while still warm. Serve warm or at room temperature, spooned onto serving plates. Serve with a spoonful of whipped cream, if desired.

**MAKES 6 TO 8 SERVINGS**

# Danish Fruit Pudding

SIMPLY THE PUREST ESSENCE of strawberries, this is the perfect dessert for when these berries are at their height. Mash them with sugar and cook them briefly with a mixture of cornstarch and water. If they aren't as sweet as you would like, add an extra tablespoon of sugar. If they need a little spark of extra flavor, add the lime juice. You can gussy the pudding up by topping it with sugared pieces of peeled ripe peaches or nectarines, blueberries and/or raspberries and drizzling with a little heavy cream.

2   pints small ripe strawberries, rinsed, hulled, halved or quartered

3   tablespoons sugar, plus more for topping

1   tablespoon plus 1 teaspoon cornstarch

1-2   teaspoons fresh lime juice (optional)

Heavy cream, plain yogurt or sour cream

1. Place the strawberries in a medium saucepan, add the 3 tablespoons sugar and mash with a potato masher. Let stand for 10 minutes. Meanwhile, stir the ½ cup water and the

cornstarch together in a small bowl until thoroughly blended and there are no lumps. Add to the berry mixture.

2. Cook over medium heat, stirring, until the mixture boils and becomes transparent, about 3 minutes. Remove from the heat and add the lime juice, if using.

3. Spoon the pudding into a pretty serving bowl or individual dessert bowls. Refrigerate until chilled, about 1 hour. Serve with a topping of whipped heavy cream, yogurt or sour cream (my favorite).

MAKES 4 SERVINGS

# Œ

# English Sticky Toffee Pudding

Tᴴɪꜱ ᴅᴇʟɪᴄɪᴏᴜꜱʟʏ ᴍᴏɪꜱᴛ, ᴅᴇᴄᴀᴅᴇɴᴛ, cakelike pudding is topped with a toffee sauce, broiled and served with more of the toffee sauce poured on top. According to the late cookbook writer Jane Grigson, the popular English pudding was invented by a country hotel operator, Francis Coulson. It's so wonderful that I think Mr. Coulson should be proclaimed a national treasure, if he hasn't been already.

1 cup plus 1 tablespoon all-purpose
  flour
1 teaspoon baking powder
¾ cup (about 4 ounces) pitted dates
1 teaspoon baking soda
4 tablespoons unsalted butter, softened
¾ cup sugar
1 large egg, lightly beaten
1 teaspoon vanilla extract

### Toffee Sauce

8 tablespoons unsalted butter
½ cup heavy cream
1 cup packed light brown sugar

1 cup heavy cream, chilled

1. Preheat the oven to 350°F, with a rack in the center. Butter a 10-inch round or 8-inch square baking dish.

2. Sift the flour and baking powder onto a sheet of waxed paper. Finely chop the dates. Place them in a small bowl and add 1¼ cups boiling water and the baking soda; set aside.

3. Beat the butter and sugar in a large bowl with an electric mixer until light and fluffy. Beat in the egg and vanilla until blended. Gradually beat in the flour mixture. Add the date mixture to the batter and fold with a rubber spatula until blended. Pour into the baking dish.

4. Bake until the pudding is set and firm on top, about 35 minutes. Transfer to a wire rack.

5. **Make the toffee sauce:** Combine the butter, heavy cream and brown sugar in a small, heavy saucepan and heat to boiling, stirring constantly. Boil gently over medium-low heat until thickened, about 8 minutes.

6. Preheat the broiler. Spread about ⅓ cup of the sauce evenly over the pudding. Place the pudding under the broiler until the topping is bubbly, about 1 minute. Spoon the pudding into dessert bowls. Beat the chilled cream with an electric mixer until soft peaks form. Drizzle each serving with more toffee sauce and top with a spoonful of whipped cream.

MAKES 8 SERVINGS

# Fig Panna Cotta

THE ITALIAN NAME, *panna cotta*, is a much more poetic way to describe this restaurant-menu favorite than the plain English translation, "cooked cream." A puree of dried figs flavors the cream.

| | | |
|---|---|---|
| **About 6 ounces dried Calimyrna figs** | | **Raspberry Sauce** |
| ¼ | cup sugar | 1 pint fresh raspberries |
| 2 | teaspoons unflavored gelatin | ¼ cup sugar |
| 1 | cup milk | |
| 1 | cup heavy cream | ½ pint fresh raspberries for garnish |
| 1 | teaspoon vanilla extract | |

1. Using kitchen scissors, snip off and discard the woody stems of the figs. Snip the figs into small (¼-inch) pieces and measure 1 cup packed. Transfer to a medium saucepan. Add 1 cup water and the sugar and heat to boiling. Cover and cook over low heat, stirring occasionally, until the figs are very soft and have absorbed all but about 2 tablespoons of the water, about 25 minutes.

2. Meanwhile, place ¼ cup water in a small bowl and sprinkle the gelatin on top.

Let stand until softened. Heat the milk in a small saucepan until hot. Remove from the heat. Add the gelatin and stir until dissolved.

3. Gradually stir the milk mixture into the hot fig mixture; cool until lukewarm. Add the heavy cream. Set a sieve over a large bowl. Using the back of a large spoon, press the mixture through the sieve. Make sure to scrape the juices from the underside of the sieve into the bowl. Discard the seeds. Stir in the vanilla.

4. Divide the panna cotta evenly among four 5-ounce custard cups. Place on a tray, cover with plastic wrap and refrigerate until set, about 3 hours or longer.

5. **Meanwhile, make the raspberry sauce:** Puree the raspberries and the sugar in a food processor. Strain to remove the seeds. Refrigerate until ready to serve.

6. To serve, quickly dip the custard cups in hot water. Loosen the edges of the panna cotta, using the tip of a knife. Place a serving plate on top of each custard cup and invert, shaking the panna cotta loose from the cup. Spoon some of the raspberry sauce around the edges of each panna cotta and garnish with whole raspberries.

Makes 4 servings

# Gram's Lemon Pudding

T HE BATTER of this old-fashioned lemon
sponge pudding separates while it bakes,
forming a soft spongy layer on top and
a tender custard on the bottom. It
comes from my friend Pat Vacca
of Corning, New York, who got
it from her grandmother. Pat
makes it in a pie crust, but I
like it baked in individual
glass custard cups so that
you can see the two layers
clearly through the sides.

½  cup sugar

2  teaspoons grated lemon zest

¼  cup fresh lemon juice

2  large eggs, *separated*

2  tablespoons all-purpose flour

1  tablespoon unsalted butter,
   melted

1  cup milk

1. Preheat the oven to 350°F, with a rack in the center. Heat a kettle of water to boiling. Generously butter four 5-ounce custard cups. Arrange them in a 13-x-9-inch baking pan.

2. Combine the sugar, lemon zest, lemon juice, egg yolks, flour and butter in a medium bowl and whisk until smooth. Add the milk and stir to blend.

3. Beat the egg whites in a clean bowl with an electric mixer until soft peaks form. Gently fold the whites into the lemon mixture until blended.

4. Pour the batter into the custard cups. Place the baking pan in the oven and carefully add enough boiling water to come halfway up the sides of the cups.

5. Bake until the puddings are lightly browned and set on top, about 30 minutes. Cool in the water bath. Serve warm or cold.

MAKES 4 SERVINGS

# H

## Honey Vanilla Mousse

THE DISTINCTIVE TASTE of honey pervades this exceptionally easy mousse. Orange-blossom honey from the supermarket is delicious, but you might want to try other honeys from more exotic blossoms, such as chestnut or eucalyptus. For the fruit surrounding the mousse, you can use peaches, nectarines, seedless grapes, sectioned seedless oranges, strawberries or a mixture of whatever is in season.

1   envelope unflavored gelatin
1   cup milk
½   cup honey
1   teaspoon vanilla extract
1   cup heavy cream

2   cups fruit, sweetened
    with approximately
    2 tablespoons honey

1. Place ½ cup cold water in a small bowl and sprinkle the gelatin on top. Let stand until softened, about 5 minutes. Heat the milk and honey in a small saucepan, stirring, until warm. Add the gelatin mixture and cook over low heat, stirring, until the gelatin dissolves, 3 to 5 minutes. Remove from the heat. Stir in the vanilla.

2. Beat the cream in a large bowl with an electric mixer until it forms soft peaks. Refrigerate until ready to use.

3. Transfer the honey mixture to a medium bowl and set over a larger bowl filled with ice and water. Chill, stirring frequently, until the mixture turns ropy and begins to mound on a spoon.

4. Using a spatula, fold the honey mixture into the whipped cream until thoroughly blended. Transfer to a 3-cup decorative mold, six 5-ounce molds or custard cups, or a serving bowl. Cover and refrigerate until set, about 4 hours.

5. To serve, dip the molds or cups quickly in a shallow pan of warm water. Loosen the edges with the tip of a knife, place a serving plate over each mold and then invert, shaking the mold to loosen the mousse and unmold. Serve the molded mousse surrounded with the honey-sweetened fruit. The mousse is also very nice spooned into pretty serving bowls or stemmed glasses, topped with spoonfuls of the fruit.

MAKES 4 TO 6 SERVINGS

# Indian Pudding

LIGHTLY SPICY, dense and sweetened with molasses, this hearty, old-fashioned pudding is named for the Native Americans who first introduced ground corn to early New England colonists. The best way to enjoy the pudding is warm, with vanilla ice cream melting into it. This recipe is adapted from one developed by my friend and fellow cookbook author Joanne Hayes.

| | |
|---|---|
| 2 **cups milk** | ½ **teaspoon ground ginger** |
| ½ **cup yellow cornmeal** | ½ **teaspoon ground cinnamon** |
| 1 **large egg** | |
| ¼ **teaspoon salt** | **Vanilla ice cream** |
| ½ **cup mild molasses** | |

1. Preheat the oven to 300°F, with a rack in the center. Generously butter a 2-quart casserole or soufflé dish. Heat the milk in a heavy, medium saucepan until small bubbles appear around the edges.

2. Meanwhile, combine 1 cup water and the cornmeal in a small bowl; stir to blend. Add the egg and the salt, and whisk to combine. Add the cornmeal mixture, molasses, ginger and cinnamon to the hot milk. Cook over medium-low heat, stirring constantly, until thickened and almost boiling.

3. Pour the pudding into the casserole dish. Bake, uncovered, until the pudding is set, about 1 hour.

4. Cool slightly before serving. Spoon into bowls and top with a scoop of vanilla ice cream. The pudding is best served warm; it can be reheated in the oven or microwave.

**MAKES 6 SERVINGS**

# J

# July 4th Pudding

S UMMER PUDDING is a very British concept, but the red and blue berries and white pillows of whipped cream remind me of the Fourth of July. As the cake slowly absorbs the berry syrup, it turns a brilliant purple. This is a wonderful dessert for summer entertaining because it serves a crowd and conveniently can be made two or three days ahead.

Paula Peck's Sponge Layer
(page 47), store-bought sponge
or pound cake or 36 ladyfingers

1½ cups sugar

1 cup heavy cream, chilled
Organic edible flowers
(pansies, nasturtiums or roses)
for garnish (optional)

### Filling

8 cups (approximately 4 pints)
fresh berries (strawberries, red
currants, raspberries, blackberries,
blueberries) or any combination
of at least three types

1. If you plan to unmold the pudding, select a 6-cup soufflé dish or bowl, preferably clear glass so you can monitor the way the cake is absorbing the syrup. Or, if you plan to spoon out the pudding, select a pretty serving bowl that holds about 8 cups or more.

2. If using a soufflé dish, cut a round of cake for the bottom (this will be the top when it is turned out) and place it on the bottom of the soufflé dish. Then cut a long 3-inch-wide strip of cake and stand it around the sides. Reserve the leftover cake for the top layer. If you are using a bowl, simply cut the cake into sections and line the inside of the bowl with them, placing them very close together so the seams will not be visible when the cake swells with syrup. If using the ladyfingers, stand them along the sides of the bowl or soufflé dish, with the rounded sides facing the wall of
the dish. Line the bottom of the dish with ladyfingers.

3. **Make the filling:** Measure out the fruit, keeping the currants separate, if using. Rinse the fruits and lay them out on a kitchen towel to dry. Hull the strawberries, halve or quarter them and place in a bowl. Pull the currants from the stems.

4. Combine the sugar and 1½ cups water in a large saucepan. Heat to boiling, stirring to dissolve the sugar. Cover and boil over medium-low heat for about 5 minutes, or until syrupy.

5. If using currants, add them to the syrup and simmer until the fruit bursts, about 3 minutes. Then stir in the remaining fruits. Cover and simmer for 5 minutes; remove from the heat.

6. With a slotted spoon, spoon the warm fruit into the soufflé dish or bowl, filling it to the top; reserve the remaining syrup. Top with pieces of cake or whole ladyfingers, patching as necessary. Slowly spoon the reserved syrup over the top layer and down the sides of the bowl, pressing with the back of a spoon and slipping a knife between the cake and the sides of the bowl so that the syrup is absorbed evenly.

7. Cover the pudding with plastic wrap and place a small plate on top to weight the pudding down. Set the bowl in a pie plate or other shallow bowl to catch any syrup that may run over the sides. Transfer any leftover syrup to a small pitcher and refrigerate. Refrigerate the pudding for about 24 hours (or longer) before serving, adding small amounts of the syrup during this time.

8. To unmold, loosen the sides of the pudding using the tip of a knife. Place a deep round platter over the bowl or soufflé dish and invert. Beat the chilled cream in a medium bowl with an electric mixer until it forms soft peaks. Serve the pudding with the whipped cream. If you are serving the pudding from a bowl, pile the whipped cream on top and decorate the cream with the flowers, if desired.

MAKES 8 TO 10 SERVINGS

# Paula Peck's Sponge Layer

I've been making this simple sponge cake from Paula Peck's *The Art of Fine Baking* for more than 20 years. It can be made several days ahead and frozen, or it can be made one day ahead, covered with plastic wrap and stored at room temperature until ready to use.

| | |
|---|---|
| 4 large eggs, *separated* | ½ teaspoon vanilla extract |
| Pinch of salt | ¼ cup sifted cornstarch |
| ¼ cup sugar | ¼ cup sifted all-purpose flour |

1. Preheat the oven to 400°F, with a rack in the center. Lightly butter an 11-x-16-inch sheet pan. Line with waxed paper. Lightly butter the waxed paper and sprinkle with flour; shake off excess.

2. Beat the egg whites and salt in a large bowl with an electric mixer until soft peaks form. Gradually beat in the sugar, 1 tablespoon at a time, until the whites form stiff peaks, about 5 minutes.

3. Meanwhile, in a separate bowl, stir the egg yolks until blended. Add the vanilla and stir to blend. Add a spoonful of the egg whites to the yolks and, using a rubber spatula, gently fold them together until well blended. Then pour the yolk mixture over the whites in the larger bowl. Sift the cornstarch and flour onto the whites and yolks. With the spatula, gently but thoroughly fold until no whites show. Do not overmix.

4. Spread the batter evenly in the pan. Bake until lightly browned, 10 to 12 minutes. Do not overbake. Remove the pan from the oven and immediately loosen the sides of the cake with a small spatula. Turn the cake out on a wire rack while it is still warm. Do not peel off the waxed paper until the cake is cooled.

MAKES 1 SPONGE LAYER, ABOUT ¾ INCH THICK

# Kugel
## (Savory Noodle Pudding)

KUGEL IS A PUDDING that is traditionally served on the Jewish Sabbath. This one is delicious for lunch or dinner made with pasta bow ties or with flat noodles, if preferred. It is even better when made ahead and reheated, and it's great for feeding a hungry crowd.

2    slices firm white bread

3    cups (about 6 ounces) bow-tie pasta

4    tablespoons unsalted butter

2    cups chopped onion

8    ounces (about 3 cups) sliced
      mushrooms
      Salt and freshly ground black pepper

1    bunch (10 ounces) fresh spinach,
      washed and trimmed, or 10 ounces
      chopped frozen spinach, cooked

6    large eggs

1    container (16 ounces) small-curd
      whole-milk cottage cheese

1    cup milk

¾    cup sour cream

1    tablespoon all-purpose flour

1½    teaspoons salt

¼    teaspoon freshly grated nutmeg

1. Tear the bread into pieces and place in a food processor. Process until fine crumbs are formed; set aside.

2. Cook the bow ties in boiling salted water until tender, 12 to 15 minutes; drain and set aside.

3. Melt 2 tablespoons of the butter in a large skillet. Add the onions and mushrooms and cook, stirring, over medium-high heat until the onions are golden and the mushrooms

are soft and lightly browned, about 10 minutes. Add salt and pepper to taste and set aside.

4. If using fresh spinach, steam it over boiling water just until wilted, about 2 minutes. Drain and cool fresh or frozen spinach, squeeze dry, then blot with a clean kitchen towel to make sure all excess water is pressed out. Coarsely chop fresh spinach.

5. Beat the eggs in a large bowl until frothy. Stir in the cottage cheese, milk, sour cream, flour, salt and nutmeg. Stir in the bow ties, the onion-mushroom mixture and the spinach.

6. Preheat the oven to 350°F, with a rack in the center. Heat a kettle of water to boiling. Lightly butter a shallow 13-x-9-inch baking dish. Set the baking dish in a larger baking pan. Spoon the kugel into the baking dish.

7. Melt the remaining 2 tablespoons butter in a small skillet. Add the bread crumbs and toss to coat. Sprinkle evenly over the top of the kugel. Place the baking pan in the oven and carefully add enough boiling water to come halfway up the sides of the baking dish.

8. Bake until the top is golden and the pudding is set, about 45 minutes. Serve warm, cut into squares.

MAKES 8 SERVINGS

# Lemon Custard Rice Pudding

T HIS BAKED RICE PUDDING from my grandmother Antoinette Abbruzzese was one of my
favorite dishes of childhood. Fortunately, my
mother preserved Nana's tattered handwrit-
ten book so subsequent generations could
enjoy the pudding. The soft grains of rice
are enveloped in a tender egg custard in-
fused with lemon zest. The pudding can
be cut into big squares and served with
a wide spatula, which is the way Nana
did. The amount of rice will alter the
firmness. For a more custardy version,
use 1½ cups cooked rice. For a stiffer
result, use up to 3 cups rice. The pudding can be made with regular long-
or medium-grain rice or Arborio.

1½-3 cups cooked long-grain or medium-
     grain white rice (from ½-1 cup raw)
  6 cups milk
  7 large eggs

1 cup sugar
1 tablespoon grated lemon zest
2 teaspoons vanilla extract
   Freshly grated nutmeg

1. Preheat the oven to 325°F, with a rack in the center. Heat a kettle of water to boiling. Butter a 13-x-9-inch baking dish and set it in a larger pan.

2. Spread the rice in the baking dish. Heat the milk in a large saucepan until small bubbles appear around the edges.

3. Beat the eggs and sugar in a large bowl with a whisk or an electric mixer until foamy. Gradually stir the hot milk into the eggs until blended. Add the lemon zest and vanilla.

4. Pour half the milk mixture into the baking dish and gently stir to combine with the rice. Carefully pour the remaining milk mixture into the baking dish. Sprinkle the top evenly with the nutmeg.

5. Place the baking dish in the oven and carefully add enough boiling water to come halfway up the sides of the baking dish. Bake until the custard is almost set and the edges are golden, about 1 hour and 15 minutes. Cool the pudding in the water bath. Spoon or cut into squares and serve at room temperature or chilled.

MAKES ABOUT 8 SERVINGS

# Lemon Crème Brûlée

C RÈME BRÛLÉE'S APPEAL comes from the dramatic contrast of the silken, creamy pudding with the glassy crackling caramelized sugar glaze. This simple lemon-and-vanilla-bean-infused version is my favorite rendition of this classic dessert.

| | |
|---|---|
| 2 cups heavy cream | 5 egg yolks |
| ½ cup sugar | |
| 1 tablespoon grated lemon zest | 4 tablespoons sugar, preferably |
| ½ vanilla bean, split lengthwise | superfine, for topping |

1. Preheat the oven to 325°F, with a rack in the center. Heat a kettle of water to boiling. Arrange six 12-ounce ramekins in a 13-x-9-inch pan or arrange six 4-inch-wide fluted flan dishes in two 13-x-9-inch pans.

2. Heat the cream, sugar, lemon zest and vanilla bean in a saucepan until small bubbles appear around the edges. Cover and let stand for 10 minutes. Place a sieve over a medium bowl and strain the mixture. Lay the vanilla bean on a flat surface and scrape the tiny seeds from the pod. Add the seeds to the lemon-infused cream

3. Stir the egg yolks in a medium bowl until blended. Gently whisk in the warm cream; do not whisk too vigorously.

4. Divide the cream evenly among the ramekins or flan dishes. Place the pan or pans in the oven and add enough boiling water to come halfway up the sides of the ramekins.

5. Bake until the custards are set in the center when the pan is gently shaken, 30 to 35 minutes for the ramekins and 20 to 25 minutes for the flan dishes. Remove the custards from the hot water and cool to room temperature. Cover and refrigerate until very cold, several hours or overnight.

6. About 20 minutes before serving, preheat the broiler. Remove the custards from the refrigerator and carefully blot any moisture from the tops with a paper towel. Place 2 or 3 custards on a baking sheet. Using a small spoon, sprinkle a thick layer of sugar (about 2 teaspoons for each one) on top. Broil about 4 inches from the heat, turning the baking sheet constantly, until the sugar is melted and evenly caramelized, 1 to 3 minutes, depending on the heat of the broiler. Repeat with the remaining custards. Let stand for a few minutes to let the sugar harden before serving.

**MAKES 6 SERVINGS**

## Mango Pudding with Blueberries

THIS PRETTY PALE ORANGE dessert is somewhere between a mousse and a pudding. The texture is soft and light, and the flavor sparkles with the fresh taste of tropical fruit. The contrast of the mango against the dark blueberries is striking to both the eye and the palate.

½ cup milk

1 envelope unflavored gelatin

2-3 large ripe mangoes

1-2 teaspoons fresh lime juice

1 cup whole-milk yogurt or ½ cup
yogurt and ½ cup sour cream

½ pint blueberries, rinsed
Blueberry Sauce (page 57)

1. Place the milk in a medium saucepan and sprinkle the gelatin on top. Let stand until softened, about 10 minutes.

2. Meanwhile, cut the mangoes in half by slicing them just off center on either side of the large flat pit. Using a tablespoon, scoop the flesh from the skin and place in a food processor. Then cut the skin from around the flesh near the pit; place the pit on a cutting board and cut away the flesh. Puree the mango (you should have about 2½ cups). Using a sieve or Foley food mill set over a bowl, strain the puree to remove any strings. Discard the solids. Stir the lime juice to taste into the mango puree.

3. Warm the milk over low heat, stirring, just until the gelatin is dissolved. Remove from the heat. Stir in the mango puree until well blended. Place a sieve over a medium bowl and strain the mixture into the bowl.

4. Place the saucepan in a bowl of ice water and let stand, stirring often, until the mango mixture is chilled enough to mound on a spoon.

5. Whisk the yogurt or yogurt–sour cream mixture in a small bowl until smooth. Fold into the mango mixture with a rubber spatula until no trace of white is visible.

6. Pour pudding into a large serving bowl or individual bowls, custard cups, or wineglasses. Serve topped with blueberries or, if desired, with blueberry sauce. Or, for a more dramatic presentation,

chill the custard cups, then place a serving plate on top of each cup and shake the pudding loose from the cup. Spoon the berries or sauce around the pudding.

MAKES 4 TO 6 SERVINGS

# Fresh Blueberry Sauce

⅓ cup sugar

1 tablespoon cornstarch

1 pint (about 2 cups) blueberries, rinsed and sorted

½ teaspoon grated lemon zest (optional)

1. Stir the sugar and cornstarch together in a medium saucepan until thoroughly blended. Add the blueberries.

2. Heat the blueberries, stirring constantly, over medium-low heat until they soften and the mixture thickens, about 5 minutes. Remove from the heat. Stir in the lemon zest, if using. Serve either at room temperature or chilled.

MAKES ABOUT 1¾ CUPS

# Malted-Milk Chocolate Pudding

T HIS PUDDING, featuring a classic combination, was inspired by Barbara Chernetz, friend and food editor. It tastes like a malted-milk ball: creamy milk chocolate dissolving on the tongue, accompanied by the seductive nutty taste of malt. Malted-milk powder comes in jars and is sold in most well-stocked supermarkets.

½ cup Carnation's Original chocolate
   malted-milk powder
¼ cup sugar
1½ tablespoons cornstarch

2 cups milk
5 ounces milk chocolate, chopped
1 egg yolk
½ teaspoon vanilla extract

1. Combine the malted-milk powder, sugar and cornstarch in a medium saucepan, and stir until thoroughly blended. Gradually stir in the milk until blended. Cook over medium-low heat, stirring gently, until the milk boils and the mixture thickens. Add the milk chocolate. Cook, stirring, until melted.

2. Beat the egg yolk in a small bowl until blended. Gradually add some of the hot-milk mixture to the egg yolk and whisk to blend. Pour the egg mixture back into the saucepan, stirring constantly. Cook over low heat, stirring, until the pudding is thick and smooth and reaches 160°F.

3. Remove from the heat and stir in the vanilla. Pour into 4 or 5 individual pudding dishes or custard cups. Serve warm, at room temperature or cold.

MAKES 4 TO 5 SERVINGS

## Nadia's Russian Cream Dessert with Red Plum Sauce

W HEN I MOVED from New York to California a few years ago, my friend Nadia Merzliakov drove across the country with me, and for the two weeks on the road, we talked about food. Somewhere en route, she described this easy pudding made with sour cream. If plums aren't in season, serve in the Russian tradition with good-quality jarred plums or cherries in heavy syrup. It will be equally grand.

1 cup heavy cream

½ cup sugar

1 envelope unflavored gelatin

1 cup sour cream

½ teaspoon vanilla extract

Red Plum Sauce (below) or
preserved (canned) red plums
in heavy syrup, pitted

1. Combine the cream, sugar and gelatin in a small saucepan and let stand for 5 minutes to soften the gelatin. Heat, stirring, until the cream is hot and the sugar and gelatin are dissolved. Set the pan over a bowl of ice water and cool, stirring often, until the cream is thick enough to mound slightly on a spoon.

2. Meanwhile, put the sour cream in a small bowl and stir until smooth. Add the vanilla. Add to the thickened cream and gently fold until combined. Pour into a medium bowl. Cover and refrigerate until set, about 2 hours.

3. To serve, spoon into serving bowls and top with the plum sauce or plums in syrup.

# Red Plum Sauce

1½ pounds fresh red plums, pitted,
cut into ½-inch chunks

¼ cup sugar, or more to taste

2 teaspoons fresh lime juice, or to taste

Combine the plums and the ¼ cup sugar in a medium saucepan. Heat over low heat, stirring, adding a little water by teaspoonfuls if the plums do not release their juices. Continue to cook, stirring, until the plums are softened, about 15 minutes. Cool slightly. Add the lime juice. Taste and add more sugar and/or lime juice, if desired. If a smooth sauce is preferred, puree in a food processor. Serve chilled.

MAKES ABOUT 2 CUPS

# Onion Custards

T HESE SAVORY CUSTARDS are sweet
with the caramelized flavor of slowly
cooked onion. I like to serve them as a
side dish with grilled fish or poultry or
as the centerpiece of an all-vegetable
supper. They are especially good unmolded
in the center of lightly dressed salad greens.
Serve them warm from the oven or make
them ahead and reheat.

| | |
|---|---|
| About 2 pounds large sweet onions (such as Vidalias or Texas Sweets) | 4 slices bacon (optional) |
| 2 tablespoons unsalted butter | 1½ cups milk |
| 1 tablespoon fresh thyme leaves, finely chopped | ½ cup heavy cream |
| 1 teaspoon kosher salt | 2 large eggs |
| Generous grindings of black pepper | 2 large egg yolks |
| | 12 small sprigs fresh thyme |

1. Peel the onions and halve them from top to bottom. Place the onions on the cut side and slice thinly into half circles. Measure out 6 cups. Melt the butter in a large, heavy skillet over medium heat. When the foam subsides, add the onions. Cover and cook over medium-low heat until wilted, about 15 minutes. Uncover and continue cooking over medium heat, stirring often and adjusting the heat so the onions brown slowly, until they are a dark golden brown and very tender, about 20 minutes. Stir in the chopped thyme, salt and pepper.

2. Meanwhile, in a large, heavy skillet, cook the bacon, if using, until the fat is rendered and the bacon is crisp. Drain. Finely chop and set aside.

3. Preheat the oven to 350°F, with a rack in the center. Heat a kettle of water to boiling. Generously brush six 5-ounce custard cups with softened butter. Arrange them in a 13-x-9-inch baking pan.

4. Heat the milk and cream in a saucepan until small bubbles appear around the edges. In a large bowl, whisk the eggs and egg yolks until blended. Slowly add the milk mixture, whisking gently until blended. Set a sieve over a large measuring cup and strain the custard into the cup. 5. Using tongs, distribute the sautéed onions evenly among the custard cups (they should be about one-quarter filled). Add the bacon, if using, distributing evenly. Add the custard, distributing evenly. Run a knife through each so that the custard will seep through the layer of onion.

6. Place the baking pan in the oven and carefully add enough boiling water to come 1 inch up the sides of the cups. Bake until the custards are lightly browned and set, about 25 minutes. Remove the pan from the oven. Using a spatula and protecting your hand with a pot holder, transfer the custard cups to a wire rack. Serve warm or at room temperature. The custards can be made ahead and reheated, several at a time, in the microwave or wrapped in foil and reheated in a low (300°F) oven.

**MAKES 6 SERVINGS**

# Pistachio Pots de Crème

S ERVE THESE VERY ELEGANT, rich puddings, which are the color of lime, for your next dinner party. The term *pots de crème* describes the ceramic cups with lids in which these custards are baked and served. As I don't have the bona fide article, I use porcelain custard cups and cover them while they are baking. The custards have a meltingly smooth taste, and they can be made a day ahead and served from the refrigerator.

Look for pistachios that are already shelled and peeled. Unpeeled pistachios are covered with a thin reddish skin, and blanching and peeling them is time-consuming.

1 **cup (8 ounces) shelled,**
  **peeled unsalted pistachios**
2 **cups heavy cream**
1 **cup milk**

⅓ **cup sugar**
¼ **teaspoon almond extract**
7 **large egg yolks**
  **Whipped cream, for topping**

1. Finely grind the nuts in a food processor or with a Mouli hand grater. Set aside ¼ cup for garnish. Heat the cream and milk in a saucepan until small bubbles appear around the edges. Stir in the ¾ cup ground nuts. Remove from the heat. Cover and let stand for 30 minutes. Set a sieve over a medium bowl and strain, pressing on the nuts to extract as much of the essence as possible. Scrape off the underside of the sieve with a rubber spatula.

2. Preheat the oven to 350°F, with a rack in the center. Heat a kettle of water to boiling. Arrange six 5-ounce custard cups in a 13-x-9-inch baking pan.

3. Add the sugar and almond extract to the warm-milk mixture and stir gently to dissolve the sugar. Place the egg yolks in a medium bowl and stir to combine. Gradually stir in the warm milk; stir gently so foam does not form. Set a clean sieve over a 4-cup glass measuring cup and strain the custard into it.

4. Pour the pistachio custard into the custard cups, dividing evenly. Place the baking pan in the oven and carefully add enough boiling water to come halfway up the sides of the cups. Cover the cups lightly with a large sheet of aluminum foil and set a cookie sheet on top of the foil to hold it down.

5. Bake until the custards are set around the edges and almost set in the center, 25 to 30 minutes. Carefully remove the baking sheet and remove the pan from the oven. Using a spatula and protecting your hand with a pot holder, transfer the custards to a wire rack to cool. Cover with plastic wrap and refrigerate until thoroughly chilled, at least 4 hours or overnight.

6. To serve, top the custards with a spoonful of softly whipped cream and garnish with the reserved ground pistachios.

**MAKES 6 SERVINGS**

# Polenta Pudding with Creamy Fig Sauce

ENRICHED WITH MASCARPONE, an Italian cream cheese, this cornmeal pudding emerges from the oven puffed and light. It will settle as it cools. I like it best served warm with fresh fruit, but it tastes fine when it is at room temperature. I often warm up the leftovers and eat them for breakfast. The recipe was inspired by one made by Joanne Weir, a fellow cookbook author.

| | |
|---|---|
| 3 cups milk | 1 teaspoon vanilla extract |
| ⅔ cup fine cornmeal | Confectioners' sugar |
| ½ teaspoon salt | |
| 4 large eggs | Creamy Fig Sauce (page 66), fresh |
| ⅓ cup sugar | figs in season, or a mixture of figs, |
| 1 cup mascarpone cheese | peaches, strawberries, blueberries |
| 1 teaspoon grated lemon zest | or raspberries |

1. Heat the milk in the top of a double boiler directly over low heat. Slowly whisk in the cornmeal. Cook, stirring constantly, until the milk boils and the polenta thickens, about 10 minutes. Do not leave unattended. Add the salt. Place the top over 2 inches of gently simmering water, cover and cook, without disturbing, for 30 minutes, replenishing the water in the bottom if necessary.

2. Meanwhile, in a large bowl, whisk the eggs and sugar until light in color. When the polenta is ready, remove the top of the double boiler from the heat and stir in the mascarpone until blended. Pour a small amount of the hot polenta into the eggs. Then whisk in the remaining polenta. Add the lemon zest and vanilla.

3. Preheat the oven to 350°F, with a rack in the center. Lightly butter a shallow 2-quart baking dish or a deep pie plate. Sprinkle with a little sugar. Add the pudding. Bake until the top is puffed and the pudding is golden around the edges, about 45 minutes.

4. Sprinkle the pudding with confectioners' sugar before serving. Serve warm or at room temperature, spooned into shallow dessert bowls and topped with fig sauce or fresh fruit.

# Creamy Fig Sauce

**About 6 ounces dried Calimyrna figs**

¼ **cup sugar**

1 **strip (½ x 2 inches) lemon or orange zest**

1 **cup heavy cream**

1 **cup milk**

½ **teaspoon vanilla extract**

1. Using kitchen scissors, snip off and discard the woody stems of the figs. Snip the figs into small (¼-inch) pieces and measure 1 cup packed. Transfer to a saucepan. Add 1 cup water, the sugar and zest and heat to boiling

2. Cover and cook over low heat, stirring occasionally, until the figs are very soft and all but about 2 tablespoons of the water is absorbed, about 25 minutes. Add small amounts of water, if necessary, to keep the figs moist. Cool slightly. Discard the zest.

3. Transfer the figs and the remaining cooking liquid to a food processor and puree. Combine the puree, cream and milk in a bowl and stir to blend. Set a sieve over another bowl and press the mixture through to remove the seeds. Discard the solids. Add the vanilla to the sauce. Serve cold or at room temperature.

**MAKES ABOUT 2 CUPS**

# Queen of Puddings

THIS CLASSIC early British recipe represents the genre of pudding at its very best. It is adapted from Jane Grigson's book *English Food*. The base is a custard, which is baked until set. A layer of jam is spread on the surface of the custard and it is piled high with whipped egg whites, which are then baked until lightly browned. The result is delicately sweet and seductive, much like lemon meringue pie without the crust.

| | |
|---|---|
| 5 slices firm white bread | 4 large eggs, *separated* |
| 2½ teaspoons grated lemon zest | 1 teaspoon vanilla extract |
| ½ cup plus 2 tablespoons sugar, plus 1 teaspoon for sprinkling | 3 tablespoons black currant or strawberry jelly |
| 2 cups milk | |
| 4 tablespoons unsalted butter | Heavy cream |

1. Tear the bread into pieces and place in a food processor. Process until fine crumbs are formed; you should have 2½ cups.

2. Place the crumbs in a bowl and add the zest and 2 tablespoons of the sugar. Combine the milk and butter in a small saucepan. Heat just until steaming and the butter is melted; do not boil. Add the milk mixture to the crumb mixture and stir to blend. Let stand for 10 minutes.

3. Preheat the oven to 350°F, with a rack in the center. Lightly butter a 9-inch pie plate or other 2-quart shallow baking dish.

4. Add the egg yolks and vanilla to the crumb mixture and whisk until blended. Pour into the pie plate or baking dish and bake until the edges are golden and the custard is firm in the center, about 25 minutes. Remove from the oven.

5. Heat the jelly in a small saucepan, stirring, just until smooth. Spoon over the custard and gently spread in an even layer.

6. In a large bowl, beat the egg whites with an electric mixer until stiff peaks form. Gradually beat in the ½ cup sugar until the whites are shiny. Drop spoonfuls of the whites onto the pudding, distributing evenly; spread with a small spatula, forming pretty peaks. Sprinkle with the remaining 1 teaspoon sugar.

7. Return the pudding to the oven and bake until the meringue is golden brown. Serve hot or warm with plenty of heavy cream.

MAKES 6 SERVINGS

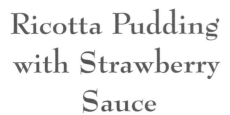

# Ricotta Pudding with Strawberry Sauce

**M**ADE SIMPLY FROM RICOTTA, eggs and sugar, this pudding of Italian origin is reminiscent of a soufflé and, like many Italian desserts, is not too sweet. I like to serve it with sugared berries—blueberries, strawberries and raspberries—or a fresh berry sauce. In a pinch, make a sauce from pureed and strained frozen berries.

3  large eggs, *separated*

1  container (15 ounces) ricotta, at room temperature

½  cup heavy cream

¼  cup sugar

1 teaspoon vanilla extract

Pinch of salt

Strawberry Sauce (page 70)

1. Preheat the oven to 350°F, with a rack in the lowest position. Heat a kettle of water to boiling. Lightly butter a 1½-to-2-quart soufflé dish or other round casserole dish. Set the dish in a larger baking pan and set aside.

2. Beat the egg yolks, ricotta, cream, sugar and vanilla in a large bowl with a whisk or electric mixer until well blended.

3. Beat the egg whites and salt in a clean bowl with an electric mixer until soft peaks form. Add a spoonful of the whites to the ricotta mixture and fold to lighten. Add the remaining whites, gently folding until incorporated.

4. Transfer the mixture to the soufflé dish. Place the baking pan in the oven. Carefully add enough boiling water to come halfway up the sides of the soufflé dish.

5. Bake until the pudding is puffed and golden and a knife inserted just off center comes out clean, about 45 minutes. Let cool in the water bath. Serve warm or chilled, with fresh berry sauce.

**MAKES 6 SERVINGS**

## Strawberry Sauce

| | |
|---|---|
| 1 **pint fresh strawberries, rinsed and hulled** | 2 **tablespoons sugar** |
| | 1 **tablespoon fresh lemon or lime juice** |

Slice enough berries to equal 1 cup (if the berries are large, halve them first and then slice); set aside. Quarter the remaining berries and place in a food processor with the sugar and lemon or lime juice; puree. Transfer the puree to a sieve set over a bowl and, using a rubber spatula, press the solids through the sieve. Scrape the juices from the underside of the sieve into the bowl. Add the sliced berries to the strained juice, cover and refrigerate until ready to serve. If the sauce gets too thick, thin with cold water, adding about 1 tablespoon at a time.

**MAKES ABOUT 1¾ CUPS**

# Savory Corn Pudding

ALTHOUGH THE TECHNIQUE for this dish is similar to that of a soufflé, the result is more like a pudding. It's slightly firm, with a silken texture and a soft center. Serve it for dinner at the height of corn and tomato season, with a side dish of skillet-roasted plum tomatoes garnished with fresh basil.

4   slices bacon (optional)
2½  cups fresh corn kernels
    (cut from 3-4 ears of corn)
2   cups milk
4   tablespoons unsalted butter
¼   cup all-purpose flour
4   large eggs, *separated*

¾   cup shredded aged cheddar, young
    moist Asiago, Gruyère or other
    flavorful semihard cheese
2   tablespoons finely sliced green
    tops of scallions or 1 tablespoon
    minced chives
1   teaspoon salt
⅛   teaspoon cayenne pepper

1. If using the bacon, cut it crosswise into ¼-inch slices. Fry in a hot skillet over medium heat until it is crisp and the fat has been rendered. Remove from the skillet with a slotted spoon to a double thickness of paper towels. Set aside.

2. Place 1½ cups of the corn and ½ cup of the milk in a food processor. Process to a fine puree, at least 2 to 3 minutes. Transfer to a sieve set over a small bowl and drain, pressing on the solids with the back of a spoon. Discard the solids.

3. Melt the butter in a large saucepan. Add the flour and cook, stirring, until smooth. Gradually add the corn-milk mixture and the remaining 1½ cups milk. Cook, stirring constantly, until the mixture thickens and boils, about 5 minutes. Remove from the heat.

4. Whisk the egg yolks in a medium bowl. Add about ½ cup of the hot milk mixture to the eggs and stir to blend. Then gradually whisk the yolk mixture into the milk mixture, whisking vigorously until blended. Stir in the remaining 1 cup corn kernels. You can stir in the bacon now or sprinkle it over the baked pudding later. Stir in the cheese, scallions or chives, salt and cayenne pepper.

5. Preheat the oven to 350°F, with a rack in the center. Heat a kettle of water to boiling. Lightly butter an 8-cup soufflé dish. Set the dish in a larger baking pan.

6. Beat the egg whites in a large bowl with an electric mixer until soft peaks form. Add a heaping spoonful of the corn mixture to the whites and gently fold until incorporated. Add the remaining corn mixture and fold until thoroughly incorporated. Pour into the soufflé dish.

7. Place the baking pan in the oven. Carefully add enough boiling water to come halfway up the sides of the soufflé dish. Bake the pudding until the top is puffed and a knife inserted just off center comes out clean, about 35 minutes.

8. Serve hot. If you chose not to incorporate the bacon into the soufflé, pass the crispy bits and sprinkle over each serving of pudding.

**MAKES 4 SERVINGS AS A MAIN COURSE, 6 AS A SIDE DISH**

# Steamed Ginger & Cranberry Pudding

S TEAMED PUDDINGS are made from a moist cake batter that is studded with all sorts of delicious flavor-intense dried fruits. Steaming plumps the fruits and leaves the cake soft and more puddinglike than cakelike. This particular one is from friend and fellow cookbook author Helen Witty.

| | | | | |
|---|---|---|---|---|
| 1½ | cups all-purpose flour | | 2 | large eggs |
| 2 | tablespoons cornmeal | | ⅔ | cup milk |
| 3 | teaspoons baking powder | | | |
| ½ | teaspoon salt | | | Ginger Cream |
| ½ | teaspoon ground ginger | | 1 | cup heavy cream, well chilled |
| ½ | teaspoon ground cinnamon | | ½ | teaspoon vanilla extract |
| ½ | cup dried cranberries | | 1-2 | tablespoons minced crystallized ginger |
| ½ | cup chopped crystallized ginger | | | |
| ¼ | teaspoon minced or grated lemon zest | | Chopped crystallized ginger or dried | |
| 3 | tablespoons unsalted butter | | | cranberries for garnish (optional) |
| ⅔ | cup packed light brown sugar | | | |

1. Prepare a mold, using either a 1-pound coffee can or a 4-cup pudding mold. Generously butter the mold. Sprinkle with granulated sugar and shake out the excess. Place a wire rack in a pot deep enough to hold the mold with the pot cover in place. Heat a kettle of water to boiling.

2. Sift the flour, cornmeal, baking powder, salt, ginger and cinnamon into a large bowl. Add the cranberries, ginger and zest; set aside.

3. In another large bowl, cream the butter and brown sugar with an electric mixer until fluffy. Beat in the eggs, one at a time, until well blended. Using a rubber spatula, fold in

one-third of the dry ingredients. Add half of the milk. Repeat with another third of the dry ingredients and then the remaining half of the milk. Add the remaining dry ingredients and fold just until blended. Do not overmix.

4. Transfer the mixture to the pudding mold. Clamp the lid in place or, if using a coffee can, shape a 10-inch square piece of foil over your fist and fasten it over the can with a rubber band or a piece of string. Fold the foil up over the fastener. Set the pudding on the rack in the pot and add enough boiling water to come two-thirds of the way to the rim of the mold. Cover the pot and steam the pudding, maintaining a gentle boil for 1½ hours, making sure to check the water level occasionally and add more boiling water, if needed.

5. Remove the mold from the pot and set on a wire rack. Uncover the pudding and let it rest for 5 minutes. Then unmold it onto the rack. Cover lightly with foil to keep warm until ready to serve. (The pudding can be cooled, wrapped in foil and allowed to mellow in the refrigerator for up to 1 week before serving. To reheat the refrigerated pudding, tightly wrap it in foil and bake in a preheated 300°F oven for 20 to 30 minutes, or until it is warmed through.)

6. **Make the cream:** Just before serving, beat the cream with an electric mixer until it begins to mound. Stir in the vanilla and fold in the ginger.

7. If the pudding has been steamed in a decorative pudding mold, place it decorative side up on a serving plate and serve with the ginger cream on the side. If it has been steamed in a coffee can, lay it on its side and slice it into ¾-inch rounds. Serve, topped with a spoonful of the ginger cream. Garnish with cranberries and crystallized ginger, if desired.

MAKES 6 TO 8 SERVINGS

# Toasted Coconut Tapioca Pudding

M EANT FOR TAPIOCA AND COCONUT FANS, this sumptuous tapioca pudding is enriched with both sweetened flaked coconut and coconut milk. Plan ahead, because the tapioca needs to be soaked overnight and then cooks for an hour in the top of a double boiler. The good news is that it can be made a day ahead, although I also love it warm.

⅓  cup small pearl tapioca  
2  cups whole milk  
¾  cup canned coconut milk  
   Pinch of salt  
1  cup sweetened flaked coconut  

2  large eggs  
⅓  cup sugar  
1  teaspoon vanilla extract  
   Rhubarb & Ginger in Syrup  
   (page 78, optional)  

1. Combine the tapioca and 2 cups cold water in a small bowl. Cover and let stand at room temperature for at least 8 hours or overnight; drain.

2. Place the milk and coconut milk in the top of a double boiler. Place over 2 inches of gently simmering water and heat until the milk is hot. Add the tapioca and the salt. Cover and cook, stirring occasionally and replenishing the water in the bottom if necessary, until thickened, about 1 hour.

3. Preheat the oven to 350°F, with a rack in the center. Spread ½ cup of the coconut in a shallow baking pan and bake until golden brown, stirring once, 6 to 7 minutes. Set aside.

4. Whisk together the eggs and sugar in a medium bowl. Using a rubber spatula, fold about 1 cup of the hot tapioca into the eggs; stir to blend. Gently stir the egg mixture into the tapioca mixture. Cook over gently simmering water, stirring occasionally, until the pudding is very thick and reaches 165° to 170°F, 10 to 15 minutes. Remove from the heat and fold in the ½ cup untoasted coconut and the vanilla. Spoon into a serving bowl or into individual serving dishes. Chill before serving.

5. To serve, sprinkle each serving with some of the toasted coconut, distributing evenly. Or, sprinkle the pudding in the large bowl with the toasted coconut and serve from the bowl into individual dishes. Serve topped with the rhubarb sauce, if desired.

MAKES 6 TO 8
SERVINGS

# Rhubarb & Ginger in Syrup

1   **pound rhubarb, washed, trimmed**
    **and cut into ½-inch pieces**

½   **cup sugar**
1   **tablespoon minced peeled fresh ginger**

Preheat the oven to 350°F. Combine the rhubarb, ½ cup water, the sugar and ginger in a heatproof bowl or casserole dish. Cover with foil or a lid and bake until the liquid begins to boil and the rhubarb is tender, 25 to 30 minutes. Do not stir or the rhubarb will become stringy. Cool, then refrigerate until chilled. The sauce can be made 2 to 3 days before serving.

**MAKES ABOUT 3 CUPS**

# Upside-Down Hot Fudge Sponge Pudding

I LOOKED HIGH AND LOW before I found a perfect chocolate sponge pudding. Finally I found this recipe from Kathy Lindsey, formerly the food editor of the *Times-Union* in Rochester, New York. It was her favorite dessert as a child. She writes, "It's my mother's recipe, and although it's easy to make, she always saved it for special occasions—it's very rich." The technique for making this pudding is distinctly odd: a stiff batter is spread in a pan and sprinkled with sugar, then cold water, or for a more grown-up taste strong coffee, is poured over the top. As it bakes, the cake forms on top, while the bottom is a wonderful fudgelike sauce. Magic!

| | |
|---|---|
| 1 cup all-purpose flour | 2 tablespoons butter, melted |
| 1¼ cups sugar | 1 teaspoon vanilla extract |
| 6½ tablespoons unsweetened cocoa powder | 1 cup chopped walnuts or pecans (optional) |
| 2 teaspoons baking powder | ½ cup packed light brown sugar |
| ¼ teaspoon salt | |
| ½ cup milk | Whipped cream, vanilla or coffee ice cream |

1. Preheat the oven to 350°F, with a rack in the center. Butter a 9- or 10-inch pie plate or a 9- or 10-inch square baking dish.

2. Sift the flour, ¾ cup of the sugar, 1½ tablespoons of the cocoa, the baking powder and salt into a large bowl. Add the milk, butter and vanilla. Stir until well blended. Stir in the nuts, if using. Spread in the pan.

3. Stir the brown sugar, the remaining ½ cup sugar and the remaining 5 tablespoons cocoa in a small bowl until blended. Sprinkle evenly over the top of the batter. Pour 1¼ cups water over the top.

4. Bake until the top is cakey, about 35 minutes. Serve the pudding warm with whipped cream or ice cream. Leftovers are great reheated in the microwave.

MAKES 4 TO 6 SERVINGS

# Victorian Diplomat Pudding with Dried Cherries

A LSO KNOWN AS CABINET PUDDING, Diplomat Pudding is an English pudding of ladyfingers or sponge cake studded with candied fruits and crumbled macaroons and covered with a custard mixture. So called because it was grand enough to serve for high-ranking diplomats or cabinet members, it's an elegant dessert for company, holidays and all elevated occasions. My version is based on a recipe developed by friend and fellow cookbook author Amy Cotler for *The Secret Garden Cookbook*.

81

8   dried apricot halves, plus ¼ cup
      diced dried apricots
¼   cup finely chopped candied
      orange peel
¼   cup dried cherries
¼   cup brandy or Grand Marnier
2   3-ounce packages ladyfingers
      (about 24) or Paula Peck's Sponge
      Layer (page 47)
8   macaroon cookies, crumbled
      (about 1 cup)

Custard

3   tablespoons sugar
2   teaspoons cornstarch
4   large eggs
1   egg yolk
1¾  cups milk
½   cup heavy cream
1   teaspoon vanilla extract

Heavy cream, Cinnamon Custard
Sauce or Vanilla Custard Sauce
(page 17, optional)

1. Combine the apricot halves, diced apricots, candied orange peel and dried cherries in a small bowl. Add the brandy or Grand Marnier and stir to blend. Cover with plastic wrap and let stand for about 1 hour or overnight.

2. Lightly butter the sides and bottom of a 6-cup soufflé dish. Cut a round of foil to fit in the bottom of the dish, butter the foil on both sides and set in place. Arrange the apricot halves, smooth side down, in a pattern on the foil. Place a few of the cherries between the apricots. Separate the ladyfingers and split. Stand them, rounded side out, around the sides of the soufflé dish. Make a layer of ladyfingers, tearing them to fit if necessary, on top of the fruit. Sprinkle with some of the macaroon crumbs and some of the remaining fruit. Repeat with 2 more layers of ladyfingers, macaroon crumbs and fruit, pressing down to make room for all of the ingredients until the soufflé dish is full.

3. **Make the custard:** Combine the sugar and cornstarch in a medium bowl and stir until blended. Add the eggs and egg yolk and whisk until smooth. Stir in the milk, cream and vanilla. Set a sieve over a clean bowl and strain the custard.

4. Preheat the oven to 325°F, with a rack in the center. Heat a kettle of water to boiling.

5. Pour the custard slowly and evenly over the ladyfinger mixture, pressing down gently with the back of a spoon and using a table knife to help the custard seep down the sides of the soufflé dish. (Reserve any remaining custard.) Let stand for 20 minutes until the custard is absorbed; add any leftover custard to fill the dish to the top. Butter one side of a piece of foil and place it buttered side down on the pudding. Fold down the edges and fasten tightly in place with cotton string.

6. Place a folded kitchen towel in a 13-x-9-inch baking pan. Set the soufflé dish on top of the kitchen towel. Place the pan in the oven and add enough boiling water to come halfway up the sides of the soufflé dish. Bake until the custard is set, about 1½ hours.

7. Remove the pudding from the water bath. Remove the foil cover. Cool. Cover and refrigerate overnight, or until thoroughly chilled.

8. To serve, loosen the pudding from the sides of the dish using the tip of a knife. Place a plate on top of the pudding and invert so the dried fruit is now on top. Serve plain, with heavy cream, or with vanilla or cinnamon custard sauce, if desired.

MAKES 8 TO 10 SERVINGS

# Vanilla Wafer & Sliced Banana Pudding

A COMBINATION OF SWEET VANILLA WAFERS, fresh banana slices and a silken vanilla pudding makes this dessert a standout. Make sure to prepare it a day ahead so the vanilla wafers have time to soften and the banana aroma can flavor the whole thing.

¾  cup sugar
3   tablespoons cornstarch
    Pinch of salt
4   cups milk
3   large eggs
2   tablespoons unsalted butter,
       cut into small pieces

2    teaspoons vanilla extract
2-3  firm ripe bananas, thinly sliced
3    cups plain vanilla wafers
        (half of a 12-ounce box)
1    cup heavy cream, chilled
½    cup dried banana chips,
        finely crushed

1. Combine the sugar, cornstarch and salt in a medium saucepan; stir until thoroughly combined. Gradually add the milk, stirring, until blended. Cook over medium-low heat, stirring constantly, until the mixture is thick and creamy, about 10 minutes.

2. Whisk the eggs in a large bowl until blended. Gradually stir in the milk mixture until blended. Return to the saucepan and cook, stirring, until the mixture coats the back of a spoon heavily and reaches 165° to 170°F; do not boil. Remove from the heat and stir in the butter and vanilla. Place a sieve over a clean bowl and strain the custard while it is hot.

3. Make a layer of vanilla wafers in 6 to 8 parfait glasses or an 8-cup serving bowl. Add a layer of banana slices, then a layer of custard. Repeat, making two more layers of wafers, banana and custard, ending with the remaining custard.

4. Cover the pudding with plastic wrap and refrigerate for at least 4 hours or overnight. Beat the cream with an electric mixer until soft peaks form. Serve, topped with the cream and sprinkled with the crushed banana chips.

MAKES 6 TO 8 SERVINGS

# White Ladies Pudding

THIS DESSERT is named for a small English village called White Ladies Aston, after a twelfth century convent of Cistercian nuns who wore white habits. According to a cookbook called *Farmhouse Kitchen*, the village was renowned for the pudding. Serve it warm from the oven without any embellishments or with sliced fresh strawberries or Rhubarb & Ginger in Syrup (page 78) and a spoonful of whipped cream.

| | |
|---|---|
| 3 tablespoons unsalted butter, softened | 2 cups milk |
| ¾ cup unsweetened shredded coconut | 3 large eggs |
| 6 slices firm sandwich bread, | ⅓ cup sugar |
| crusts trimmed | ½ teaspoon vanilla extract |

1. Generously butter a 10-inch pie plate or 10-inch square baking dish with some of the softened butter. Sprinkle with ½ cup of the coconut.

2. Spread the slices of bread generously with the remaining softened butter. Stack the slices and cut them into 4 squares. Arrange, slightly overlapping, in the pie plate or baking dish.

3. Heat the milk in a small saucepan until small bubbles appear around the edges. Whisk the eggs and sugar in a medium bowl until well blended. Slowly stir in the hot milk and stir to dissolve the sugar. Add the vanilla. Pour through a sieve over the bread. Sprinkle the top evenly with the remaining ¼ cup coconut. Let stand for 30 minutes, pressing down on the bread occasionally so it absorbs the custard evenly.

4. Preheat the oven to 350°F, with a rack in the center. Heat a kettle of water to boiling. Set the pudding in a larger baking pan. Place the baking pan in the oven and add enough boiling water to come halfway up the sides of the pie plate or baking dish.

5. Bake until the custard is set and the top is lightly browned, 30 to 35 minutes. Remove from the oven and let the pudding cool in the water bath. Serve warm or at room temperature.

MAKES 6 SERVINGS

# X-traordinarily Rich Chocolate Pudding

WHAT COULD BE MORE SIMPLE or more delicious to offer in pudding cups to kids or in elegant china cups to grown-ups? Bring out this pudding while it is still warm, or make it ahead and serve cold. Either way it is scrumptious. Serve with a spoonful of whipped cream or a drizzle of unwhipped heavy cream.

| | | | |
|---|---|---|---|
| 1 | cup milk | 5 | ounces bittersweet chocolate, |
| 1 | cup heavy cream | | preferably imported or best-quality, |
| ¼ | cup sugar | | coarsely chopped |
| 1 | tablespoon cornstarch | 2 | egg yolks |
| | Pinch of salt | 1 | teaspoon vanilla extract |

1. Heat the milk and cream in a small saucepan until small bubbles appear around the edges. Or, place in a 2-cup glass measuring cup and heat in the microwave for 2 to 3 minutes.

2. Combine the sugar, cornstarch and salt in a medium saucepan and stir until blended. Add the hot-milk mixture and heat over medium-low heat, stirring, until it begins to thicken and boil. Add the chocolate. Cook, stirring slowly and constantly, until the mixture boils and the chocolate is melted.

3. Whisk the egg yolks in a small bowl. Add a spoonful of the hot-milk mixture to the eggs

and stir to blend. Stir the egg mixture back into the saucepan. Cook over low heat, stirring, for 2 minutes, or until the pudding is thickened and reaches 165° to 170°F.

4. Set a sieve over a bowl and strain the pudding. Push the last drops of pudding through and scrape the underside of the sieve with a rubber spatula. Stir in the vanilla.

5. Transfer the pudding to a serving bowl or individual pudding cups or dessert dishes. Serve warm, at room temperature or chilled.

MAKES 4 SERVINGS

# Yogurt & Strawberry Pudding with Sugared Strawberries

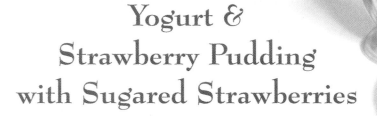

THE FLAVOR OF THIS MOUSSELIKE PUDDING is best at the height of strawberry season when the berries are sweet and juicy. Though it goes together very quickly, the pudding will need a few hours to set before serving. Garnish with more strawberries or use a combination of strawberries, raspberries and blackberries. This is also excellent with strawberry sauce (page 70) or raspberry sauce.

| | |
|---|---|
| 2 | **pints fresh strawberries** |
| 1 | **envelope unflavored gelatin** |
| 4–5 | **tablespoons sugar, or more to taste** |
| 2 | **teaspoons fresh lime juice, or more to taste** |
| 1 | **cup whole-milk or low-fat yogurt, stirred until smooth, at room temperature** |

90

1. Rinse and hull the strawberries. Cut 1 pint strawberries into quarters and place in a food processor. Slice the remaining berries and place in a medium bowl; set aside at room temperature.

2. Place ¼ cup cold water in a small bowl and sprinkle with the gelatin. Let stand until softened, about 5 minutes. Meanwhile, add 3 tablespoons sugar and 1 teaspoon lime juice to the strawberries in the food processor and puree. Place about ½ cup of the pureed mixture in a small saucepan. Add the softened gelatin and heat over medium-low heat, stirring gently, just until the puree is hot and the gelatin is dissolved. Remove from the heat.

3. Set a sieve over a medium bowl and add both pureed strawberry mixtures. Press through the sieve, using a rubber spatula. Discard the seeds and any undissolved lumps of gelatin left in the sieve.

4. Add the yogurt and gently stir until thoroughly blended. If using low-fat yogurt, taste the mixture and add 1 more tablespoon of sugar, if desired. Transfer to a serving bowl or to four 5-ounce custard cups.

5. Cover with plastic wrap and refrigerate until the pudding is set, at least 2 hours. Meanwhile, add 1 tablespoon sugar and 1 teaspoon fresh lime juice (or more of each to taste) to the reserved sliced berries. Toss to blend. Cover and let stand at room temperature until ready to serve.

6. To serve the pudding from the bowl, spoon it out into individual dessert bowls and top each with some of the sliced strawberries. Or, run a thin knife around the edges of the custard cups and quickly dip into warm water to loosen the sides. Place a dessert plate on top of each and invert. Spoon the berries around and on top of the pudding.

MAKES 4 SERVINGS

# Zucchini Parmesan Custards

T HESE DELICATE CUSTARDS are perfect as a side dish with grilled or roasted meats or poultry. I also like them unmolded and surrounded by sautéed diced zucchini, carrots and new potatoes seasoned with fresh basil.

| | |
|---|---|
| 2-3 small zucchini (about 6 ounces each) | 2 egg yolks |
| 1 tablespoon unsalted butter | ⅓ cup freshly grated Parmigiano- |
| 1 tablespoon grated onion | Reggiano cheese |
| 1½ cups milk | ½ teaspoon salt |
| ½ cup heavy cream | Pinch of freshly ground white pepper |
| 2 large eggs | |

1. Preheat the oven to 350°F, with a rack in the center. Heat a kettle of water to boiling. Arrange six 5-ounce custard cups in a 13-x-9-inch baking pan.

2. Wash and trim the zucchini. Using the coarse scalloped blade on a hand grater, shred enough zucchini to measure 1 cup packed.

3. Melt the butter in a medium skillet. Using a brush, lightly coat the inside of each custard cup with a little of the butter. Add the zucchini and the onion to the hot butter remain-

ing in the skillet. Cook the vegetables over medium heat, stirring occasionally, for 5 minutes, or until tender and the skillet is dry.

4. Heat the milk and cream in a medium saucepan until small bubbles appear around the edges. In a large bowl, whisk the eggs and yolks until blended. Slowly whisk in the hot milk mixture. Set a sieve over a large measuring cup and strain the custard mixture into it. Add the cheese, salt and pepper. Stir in the zucchini mixture.

5. Stir the custard mixture to distribute the zucchini evenly and carefully ladle it into the cups. Place the baking pan in the oven. Carefully add enough boiling water to come 1 inch up the sides of the cups. Bake until the custards are set, about 25 minutes. Remove the pan from the oven and, using a spatula and protecting your hand with a pot holder, transfer the cups to a wire rack to cool slightly.

6. Serve directly from the custard cups or run a thin knife around the edges of the cups to loosen the custard. Place a small serving plate on top of each, invert and serve.

**MAKES 6 SERVINGS**

# Index

# Puddings A *to* Z